THE WIZARD OF OZ

THE WIZARD OF OZ

L. Frank Baum
Illustrated by Charles Santore

Condensed from *The Wonderful Wizard of Oz*

With an Introduction by
Michael Patrick Hearn

JELLY BEAN PRESS

New York

The Wonderful Wizard of Oz, by L. Frank Baum, was originally published in 1900.

This 1991 edition is published by JellyBean Press, a division of dilithium Press, Ltd.,
distributed by Outlet Book Company, Inc., a Random House Company, 225 Park Avenue South,
New York, New York 10003.

DILITHIUM is a registered trademark and JELLYBEAN PRESS is a trademark of dilithium Press, Ltd.

Printed and bound in Italy

Book design by Jean Krulis

Library of Congress Cataloging-in-Publication Data

Baum, L. Frank (Lyman Frank), 1856–1919.
The wizard of Oz / by L. Frank Baum ; illustrated by Charles Santore ; with an introduction by
Michael Patrick Hearn.—1991 ed.
p. cm. "Condensed from the original text."
Summary: After a cyclone transports her to the land of Oz, Dorothy must seek out the great
wizard in order to return to Kansas.
ISBN 0-517-69506-5 (trade)   0-517-06655-6 (lib. bdg.)
[1. Fantasy.] I. Santore, Charles, ill. II. Title.
PZ7.B327Wi 1991 [Fic]—dc20 91-6901 CIP AC

1 3 5 7 8 6 4 2

To my wife, Olenka,
my dear traveling companion on that long journey
down the yellow brick road

CHARLES SANTORE

A NOTE ON THE TEXT

This book represents Charles Santore's personal vision of L. Frank Baum's inspired story. It was conceived as a highly visual interpretation, but one that would be faithful to Baum's text.

To that end, the original story has been carefully condensed, so that virtually no language other than Baum's has been used.

Donna Jo Fuller has done the condensation of the text, in collaboration with Charles Santore.

CLAIRE BOOSS
Editor

ACKNOWLEDGMENTS

Caryn Malitzky enthusiastically suggested *The Wizard of Oz* to me; I read it, and she was right. That enthusiasm never wavered over the three years it took to complete the project, and I am grateful to her.

This is the second book that I have worked on with Claire Booss. Claire is a thoughtful, thorough, and sensitive editor, and it is a pleasure to work with her. I would also like to commend Donna Jo Fuller, for doing such a great job of assisting Claire in condensing Frank Baum's wonderful text.

I am grateful to Don Bender, our perceptive Art Director, and to Jean Krulis, for striking just the right notes in her elegant design for this book. In addition, thanks are due to Sally McCravey, Director of Production, Susan Wein, and Cindy Kaye-Mizrahi, Production Supervisors, for the skillful innovation that this project demanded.

Lizzie Leonard, who acted as the model for Dorothy, is a graceful, spirited, and altogether delightful little girl. The first time I saw her, I knew I had found my inspiration for Dorothy.

I would also like to thank Michael Patrick Hearn for his generous, enthusiastic reaction to my pictures for this book.

C.S.

INTRODUCTION

I f Oz is, indeed, as Ray Bradbury has said, "what we would hope and like to be," then it is no surprise that *The Wizard of Oz* has been so frequently reinterpreted since it first appeared in 1900. L. Frank Baum was fortunate in having as his earliest collaborator William Wallace Denslow, who not only helped shoulder the costs of the book's initial publication but also insured its immediate success through his twenty-four color plates and countless lively textual decorations, establishing a tradition of lavishly illustrated editions of *The Wizard of Oz* from the start. Baum worked as closely with Denslow as Lewis Carroll did with John Tenniel, but unlike *Alice in Wonderland*, the story of *The Wizard of Oz* has long had a life apart from its original pictures. A year hardly passes now without yet another newly illustrated edition of this children's classic. It likewise has been reinterpreted on stage, screen, or television almost since the year it was published, its most famous reincarnation being the 1939 motion picture musical starring Judy Garland. And this American fairy tale has proved to be as durable abroad as at home. It is one of the most frequently translated children's books of all time, and the Russian retelling is so popular that *Elli*, the *Strashila, Zhelesnyi Drovosek, Truslivyi Lev,* and *Totoshka,* too, are as well known to Soviet schoolchildren today as Dorothy, the Scarecrow, Tin Woodman, Cowardly Lion, and Toto are to American boys and girls.

Perhaps the most opulent edition of all is the present one by Charles Santore. Like W. W. Denslow and his successor, John R. Neill, as well as Baum's successor, Ruth Plumly Thompson, Santore was born in Philadelphia. He studied at the Philadelphia Museum School of Art, where the Brandywine tradition, as best exemplified in the work of Howard Pyle and his student N. C. Wyeth, was still being kept alive by Henry C. Pitz in his classes. Here, Santore was schooled in the legacy of the "Golden Age" of American Illustration, and on graduation, he had the good fortune of landing his first editorial commission with the old *Saturday Evening Post.* Subsequent work appeared in *Ladies' Home Journal, Redbook, Cosmopolitan,* and other prominent periodicals, but, after twenty-five years as one of the country's leading commercial artists, Santore grew disenchanted with magazine and advertising assignments. He wanted to illustrate children's books. What drew him to this new field was the challenge of doing purely narrative illustration, the chance to tell a story pictorially by sustaining the characters through varying locales and dramatic incidents.

After his stunning picture book of *Aesop's Fables* came out in 1988 (also published by JellyBean Press), Santore was asked to reillustrate *The Wizard of Oz*. At first, he was not interested. He had never read Baum's book as a child, and he was not a fan of the famous movie. Although he did enjoy the music and the dancing, he was unimpressed with the sets and costumes, the midgets, and the special effects. "It was all too mechanical," he explains. "It all seemed rather hokey to me, and I thought it was probably the same with the book." But, when he finally did read *The Wizard of Oz* (and only reluctantly), it proved to be a revelation to him. "It opened itself up to me," he recalls, "providing all kinds of possibilities for dealing with people, animals, and architecture. It had everything. It was a great challenge, the biggest challenge I've ever had. And my enthusiasm began to build as I read it over and over again." But he also approached the project with some trepidation. He now had to deal with the childhood icons of so many Americans, with so many other conceptions of how the characters should look and how the story should be depicted. He also had to find a "hook," something that would define Dorothy's journey for him; and when he read that she was an "orphan," he discovered the right touch of poignancy that gave a special meaning to the fairy tale for him.

While others have treated *The Wizard of Oz* as musical comedy, Charles Santore has interpreted the story as grand opera. Never has the Kansas cyclone seemed more threatening, the Land of the Munchkins more enchanting, the forests of Oz more foreboding, the Deadly Poppy Field deadlier, or the Emerald City more magnificent than in his watercolors. And no other artist has so beautifully blended Baum's naturalism with the fantasy as has Santore in his panoramas. "What does Oz really look like?" he asked himself. "What do I think Baum himself imagined when he created Oz?" Santore decided to illustrate the story in sequence, page by page, so that he would discover the extraordinary events of the tale just as Dorothy and her friends did. "I approached the work very seriously," Santore says, "as though I were on the journey as a naturalist, recording these things for the very first time."

Santore's naturalist's sensibility, so evident in *Aesop's Fables*, served him well again when illustrating *The Wizard of Oz*. All of the creatures of Oz, from the woeful Cowardly Lion, to the most alarming of Winged Monkeys, to the little Queen of the Field Mice, in her acorn crown and oak-leaf cloak, are keenly delineated. And Baum's other characters, both the major and the seemingly insignificant, are just as vividly defined. In the Scarecrow, Santore has captured some of the marvelous loose-limbed movement of Ray Bolger's dancing; and the Tin Woodman, with his inspired watering-can head, reflects the artist's deep appreciation of American folk art. As in Baum's story, Santore's humbug wizard is all things to all people: the artist says that he had P. T. Barnum, Thomas Edison, and W. C. Fields in mind, but Oz also looks a bit like Norman Mailer! And his Wicked Witch of the West is a masterpiece of terror and comedy, unlike any previous portrayal of the old hag. While Denslow was criticized for not being able to draw a childlike child, Santore's Dorothy is a full-blooded American girl who always moves forward in pursuit of a way to get back home.

Santore also wisely has chosen not to treat *The Wizard of Oz* as a period piece. His Land of Oz is timeless, so that the Munchkins can comfortably inhabit houses reminiscent of the American colonial style, while the Emerald City is appropriately built in the art nouveau manner of the Spaniard, Antonio Gaudi. The turn of the century is also evoked through Glinda, the Good Witch, who might have graced one of Alphonse Mucha's French posters, which, by the way, also inspired Neill's depiction of Princess Ozma in the later Oz books.

To include the entire suite of sixty watercolors in *The Wizard of Oz* demanded that the text be abridged. Fortunately, the story has been condensed, rather than adapted or retold, so that almost every word that remains is Baum's own. Of course, some incidents had to be dropped. There is no Dainty China Country; and as in the movie, the Wizard disguises himself only as the Great Head rather than in a different form for each of his visitors. And what a shame there are no Kalidahs! Santore could have drawn those monsters, half tiger and half bear, brilliantly. Nevertheless, the heart and brain and courage of the original remains in this magnificent new edition. No doubt, L. Frank Baum himself would have enjoyed Charles Santore's interpretation of his American fairy tale.

MICHAEL PATRICK HEARN

Dorothy lived in the midst of the great Kansas prairies, with Uncle Henry, who was a farmer, and Aunt Em, who was the farmer's wife. Their house was small: there were four walls, a floor and a roof, which made one room; and this room contained a rusty-looking cooking stove, a cupboard for the dishes, a table, three or four chairs, and the beds. Uncle Henry and Aunt Em had a big bed in one corner, and Dorothy a little bed in another corner. There was no garret at all, and no cellar—except a small, dark hole dug in the ground, called a cyclone cellar, where the family could go in case one of those great whirlwinds arose, mighty enough to crush any building in its path. It was reached by a trapdoor in the middle of the floor.

When Dorothy stood in the doorway and looked around, she

could see nothing but the great
gray prairie on every side:
not a tree nor a house broke
the broad sweep of flat country.
The sun had baked the plowed land
into a gray mass. Once the house had
been painted, but now it was as dull
and gray as everything else.

When Aunt Em came there to live she
was a young, pretty wife, but the sun and
wind had changed her, too; they had taken
the sparkle from her cheeks and eyes and left
them gray. She never smiled. When Dorothy, who
was an orphan, first came to her, Aunt Em had been
startled by the child's laughter; whenever Dorothy's
merry voice reached her ears, she looked at the little
girl with wonder that she could find anything to laugh at.

Uncle Henry never laughed. He worked hard from morning till
night. He was gray also, from his long beard to his rough boots.

It was Toto that made Dorothy laugh. Toto was a little black dog,
with long, silky hair and twinkling black eyes. Toto played all day
long, and Dorothy played with him, and loved him dearly.

Today, however, they were not playing. Uncle Henry sat upon the
doorstep and looked anxiously at the sky. Dorothy stood in the door
with Toto in her arms, and looked at the sky, too.

From the far north they heard a low wail of the wind, and Uncle
Henry and Dorothy could see where the long grass bowed in waves
before the coming storm. There now came a sharp whistling in the
air from the south, and as they turned their eyes that way, they saw
ripples in the grass coming from that direction, also.

Suddenly Uncle Henry stood up.

"There's a cyclone coming, Em," he called; "I'll go look after the
stock." Then he ran toward where the cows and horses were kept.

Aunt Em dropped her work and came to the door. One glance
told her of the danger close at hand.

"Quick, Dorothy!" she screamed, "run for the cellar!"

Toto jumped out of
Dorothy's arms and
hid under the bed.
Aunt Em threw
open the trapdoor
and climbed down
the ladder into
the dark cellar.
Dorothy caught
Toto at last, and
started to follow her
aunt. All at once there
came a great shriek from
the wind, and the house shook
so hard that she lost her footing
and sat down suddenly on the floor.

A strange thing happened.

The house whirled around two or three
times and rose slowly through the air.
Dorothy felt as if she were going up in a
balloon. The great pressure of the wind on
every side of the house raised it up higher and
higher till it was at the very top of the cyclone;
and there it remained and was carried miles and
miles away, as easily as you could carry a feather.

It was very dark, and the wind howled horribly around her, but
Dorothy found she was riding quite easily. After the first few whirls
around, she felt as if she were being rocked gently.

Hour after hour passed, and Dorothy got over her fright; but she
felt quite lonely, and the wind shrieked loudly all about her. At first
she wondered if she'd be dashed to pieces when the house fell; but
as time passed and nothing terrible happened, she stopped worry-
ing. At last she crawled over the swaying floor to her bed and lay
down; Toto followed and lay down beside her.

In spite of the swaying of the house and the wailing of the wind,
Dorothy soon closed her eyes and fell fast asleep.

orothy was awakened by a shock. What had happened? Toto put his little nose into her face and whined. She sprang from her bed and, with Toto at her heels, ran and opened the door.

Dorothy gave a cry of amazement and looked about her, her eyes growing bigger and bigger at the wonderful sights she saw.

The cyclone had set the house down, very gently—for a cyclone—in the midst of a country of marvelous beauty. Banks of gorgeous flowers were on every hand, and birds with brilliant plumage sang in the trees and the bushes.

While she stood gazing at the strange sights, she saw coming toward her a group of very queer people. They were not as big as the grown folk she knew, nor were they very small. In fact, they seemed about Dorothy's size, although they looked much older.

The three men and one woman all were oddly dressed. They wore round hats that rose to a point, with little bells around the brims that tinkled sweetly as they moved. The men's hats were blue; the little woman's hat was white, and she wore a white gown sprinkled with little stars that glistened in the sun. The men were about as old as Uncle Henry, but the little woman was much older: her hair was nearly white, and she walked rather stiffly.

They drew near the house and the little old woman walked up to Dorothy, made a low bow, and said, "You are welcome, most noble Sorceress, to the land of the Munchkins. We are so grateful to you for having killed the Wicked Witch of the East and setting our people free from bondage."

What could she possibly mean by calling Dorothy a sorceress? And she had never killed anything!

"You are very kind, but there must be some mistake. I have not killed anything," said Dorothy.

"Your house did, anyway," said the old woman with a laugh, "and that is much the same thing. See!"

Dorothy looked, and gave a cry of fright. There under the corner of the house two feet were sticking out, shod in silver shoes.

"That's all that's left of the Wicked Witch of the East. She enslaved all the Munchkins for many years. Now they are free, and very grateful to you for the favor."

"Who are the Munchkins?" asked Dorothy of the old woman.

"They are the people who live in this land of the East."

"Are you a Munchkin?" asked Dorothy.

"No; I am the Witch of the North; but I'm a good witch." Then she laughed; the dead Witch's feet had disappeared.

All that was left were the silver shoes. "She was so old that she dried up quickly in the sun. The silver shoes are yours." She shook the dust out of them and handed them to Dorothy. "There is some charm connected with them, but what it is we never knew."

"I must go home to my aunt and uncle in Kansas," said Dorothy. "I'm sure they're worried. Can you show me the way?"

The good Witch said, "The Land of Oz is surrounded on all sides by a great desert. You must go to the City of Emeralds; it is ruled by Oz, the Great Wizard, who is more powerful than all of the Witches together. He may help you."

Dorothy asked anxiously, "How can I get there?"

"The road to the City of Emeralds is paved with yellow brick," said the Witch, "so you cannot miss it. You must walk through a country sometimes pleasant, sometimes dark and terrible. However, my magic arts can help keep you from harm. No one will dare injure a person who has been kissed by the Witch of the North." And she came close to Dorothy and kissed her gently on the forehead. Her lips left a round, shining mark. Then she whirled around on her left heel three times, and straightaway disappeared, much to little Toto's surprise. But Dorothy, knowing her to be a witch, had expected her to disappear in just that way, and was not surprised in the least.

When Dorothy was left alone, she set about making ready for the journey to the City of Emeralds.

She had only one other dress, and that was hanging on a peg beside her bed. The girl dressed herself in the clean gingham, with white and blue checks, and tied her pink sunbonnet on her head. She took a little basket and filled it with bread from the cupboard, laying a white cloth over the top. Then she looked down at her feet and noticed how worn her shoes were. "They surely will never do for a long journey, Toto," she said. And Toto looked up into her face and wagged his tail to show he knew what she meant. At that moment, Dorothy saw the silver shoes that had belonged to the Witch of the East. She said to Toto, "They would be just the thing." She took off her old leather shoes and tried on the silver ones.

They fitted her as well as if they had been made for her.

Finally, she picked up her basket.

"Come along, Toto," she said, "we will go to the Emerald City and ask the great Oz how to get back to Kansas again."

She closed the door, locked it, and put the key carefully in the pocket of her dress. And so, with Toto trotting along soberly behind her, she started on her journey.

There were several roads nearby, but it did not take her long to find the one paved with yellow brick. Within a short time she was walking briskly toward the Emerald City, her silver shoes tinkling merrily on the hard, yellow roadbed. The sun shone bright and the birds sang sweet and Dorothy did not feel nearly as bad as you might think a little girl would in a strange land. She was surprised, as she walked along, to see how pretty the country was about her. There were neat fences

at the sides of the road, painted a dainty blue color, and beyond them were fields of grain and vegetables in abundance. Once in a while, she would pass a house and the people came out to look at her and bow low as she went by, for everyone knew she had been the means of destroying the Witch. The houses of the Munchkins were odd-looking dwellings, for each was round, with a big dome for a roof. All were painted blue, for in this East country, blue was the favorite color. Toward evening, when Dorothy was tired with her long walk, she came to a house rather larger than the rest. On the green lawn before it many men and women were dancing. Five little fiddlers played as loudly as possible and the people were laughing and singing, while a big table nearby was loaded with delicious fruits and nuts, pies and cakes, and many other good things to eat.

The people greeted Dorothy kindly, and invited her to supper and to pass the night with them and to celebrate their freedom from the bondage of the Wicked Witch. Dorothy was waited upon by a Munchkin named Boq. She watched the people dance. Boq saw her silver shoes and said, "You must be a great sorceress."

"Why?" asked the girl.

"Because you wear silver shoes and have killed the Wicked Witch. Besides, you have white in your frock, and only witches and sorceresses wear white."

"My dress is blue-and-white checked," said Dorothy.

"It's kind of you to wear that," said Boq. "Blue is the Munchkin color and white is the witch color; so we know you are a friendly witch."

Dorothy didn't know what to say, for everyone seemed to think her a witch, and she knew very well she was an ordinary little girl.

When she had tired, Boq led her into the house, where he gave her a room with a pretty bed in it.

Dorothy slept soundly till morning, with Toto curled up beside her. The next morning she asked Boq how far it was to the Emerald City.

"I do not know," answered Boq, gravely, "for I have never been there. But it is a long way to the Emerald City, and it will take you many days. The country here is pleasant, but you must pass through rough and dangerous places before you reach the end of your journey."

This worried Dorothy a little, but she knew that only the great Oz could help her get to Kansas again, so she bravely resolved not to turn back.

She bade her friends goodbye, and again started along the road of yellow brick. When she had gone several miles she thought she would stop to rest, and so climbed to the top of the fence beside the road and sat down. There was a great cornfield beyond the fence, and not far away she saw a scarecrow, placed high on a pole to keep the birds from the ripe corn.

Dorothy leaned her chin upon her hand and gazed thoughtfully at the Scarecrow. Its head was a small sack stuffed with straw, with eyes, nose and mouth painted on it to represent a face.

Then Dorothy was surprised to see one of the eyes slowly wink at her. She thought she must've been mistaken, for Kansas scarecrows never wink; but presently it nodded to her in a friendly way.

"Good day," said the Scarecrow, in a rather husky voice.

"Did you speak?" asked the girl, in wonder.

"Certainly," answered the Scarecrow. "How do you do?"

"I'm pretty well, thank you," replied Dorothy. "How do you do?"

"I'm not feeling well," said the Scarecrow, with a smile, "for it is very tedious being perched up here to scare away crows."

"Can't you get down?" asked Dorothy.

"No, for this pole is stuck up my back. If you will please take away the pole, I shall be greatly obliged to you."

Dorothy lifted the figure off the pole; for, being stuffed with straw, it was quite light.

"Thank you," he said. "Who are you, and where are you going?"

"My name is Dorothy, and I am going to the Emerald City, to ask the great Oz to send me back to Kansas."

"Where is the Emerald City?" he inquired. "And who is Oz?"

"Why, don't you know?" she returned, surprised.

"No, indeed; I don't know anything. You see, I'm stuffed so I have no brains at all," he answered sadly. "Do you think, if I go to the Emerald City with you, that the great Oz would give me some brains?"

"I cannot tell," she returned; "but you may join me. If Oz won't give you any brains, you'll be no worse off than you are now."

"That is true," said the Scarecrow. "You see," he continued, confidentially, "I don't mind my body being stuffed, because I cannot get hurt. But I do not want people to call me a fool, and if my head stays stuffed with straw instead of with brains, as yours is, how am I ever to know anything?"

They walked back to the yellow brick road, and started along the path for the Emerald City. Toto sniffed and growled at the Scare-crow.

"Don't mind Toto," said Dorothy, "he never bites."

"Oh, I'm not afraid of him; all I'm afraid of is a lighted match! Tell me about where you came from," he said as they walked. So she told him all about Kansas, and how gray everything was there.

The Scarecrow could not understand why she wished to leave this beautiful country and go back to the gray place called Kansas.

"That is because you have no brains," answered the girl. "No matter how dreary and gray our homes are, people would rather live there than anywhere else. There is no place like home."

Toward evening, they came to a great forest, where the trees grew so big and close together that their branches met over the road of yellow brick and shut out the remaining daylight. They stumbled along in the darkness until the Scarecrow saw a little cottage. He led her to it, and Dorothy soon fell into a sound sleep with Toto beside her. The Scarecrow, who was never tired, stood up in a corner and waited patiently until morning came.

When Dorothy awoke, the sun was shining and Toto was

already out chasing birds and squirrels. She sat up and looked around. There was the Scarecrow, still patiently waiting for her.

They left the cottage and walked until they found a little spring, where Dorothy drank and bathed. Through the trees was a clearing by the roadside. There they sat down and Dorothy opened her basket; she offered some bread to the Scarecrow, but he refused.

"I am never hungry," he said; "and it is a lucky thing I am not. For my mouth is only painted, and if I should cut a hole in it so I could eat, the straw I am stuffed with would come out, and that would spoil the shape of my head."

Dorothy saw at once that this was true, so she nodded and asked, "Won't you tell me a story, while we are resting?"

The Scarecrow looked at her reproachfully, and answered, "My life has been so short that I really know nothing whatever. I was only made the day before yesterday. When the farmer made my head, one of the first things he did was to paint my ears, so that I could hear what was going on. Then he painted my right eye, and as soon as it was finished, I found myself looking at him and at everything around me with a great deal of curiosity, for this was my first glimpse of the world. The farmer carried me to the cornfield and set me up on a tall stick, where you found me."

Dorothy packed her basket to go; but she was startled to hear a deep groan nearby.

"What was that?" she asked timidly.

"I can't imagine," replied the Scarecrow, "but we can go and see."

They went back into the forest a few steps, then Dorothy saw standing beside one of the big trees, with an uplifted axe in his hands, a man made entirely of tin. He stood perfectly motionless, as if he could not stir at all. Toto barked sharply and made a snap at the tin legs, which hurt his teeth.

"Did you groan?" asked Dorothy.

"Yes," answered the tin man, "I did. I've been groaning for more than a year, and no one has ever heard me before or come to help me."

"What can I do for you?" she asked.

"Please get the oil can from a shelf in my cottage and oil my joints," he said.

Dorothy at once did as he asked. On her return, the Tin Woodman said, "Oil my neck first." So she oiled it, and, as it was quite badly rusted, the Scarecrow

took hold of the tin head and moved it gently from side to side until it worked freely, and then the man could turn it himself.

"Now oil the joints in my arms," he said. And Dorothy did. Finally, the Tin Woodman lowered his axe. "This is a great comfort," he said. "I have been holding that axe in the air since I rusted a year ago; now, if you will oil the joints of my legs, I'll be all right once more. I might have stood there always, if you had not come along," he said, thanking them. "How did you happen to be here?"

"We're going to Emerald City to see the great Oz," she said.

"Why do you wish to see Oz?" he asked.

"I want him to send me back to Kansas; and the Scarecrow wants him to put a few brains in his head," Dorothy replied.

The Tin Woodman appeared to think deeply for a moment. Then he said, "Do you suppose Oz could give me a heart?"

"Why, I guess so," Dorothy answered. "It would be as easy as giving the Scarecrow brains."

"Well then, if you

will allow me to join your party, I will also ask Oz to help me."

"Come along," said the Scarecrow heartily, and Dorothy agreed. So the Tin Woodman shouldered his axe and asked Dorothy to put his oil-can in her basket. They set out through the forest and the Tin Woodman said, "During the year I stood there, I had time to think that the greatest loss I had ever known was the loss of my heart. Once I was in love; but the girl I loved lived with an old woman who didn't want her to marry me, so she had the Wicked Witch of the East cast a spell on me. So now I am made all of tin, and I am very lonely; no one can love who has not a heart."

"All the same," said the Scarecrow, "I shall ask for brains instead of a heart; for a fool would not know what to do with a heart if he had one."

"Once I had brains, and a heart also; so, having tried them both, I should much rather have a heart," returned the Woodman, "for brains do not make one happy."

Dorothy and her companions walked through the thick woods where the yellow brick road was covered by dried branches and dead leaves. Now and then, there came a deep growl from some wild animal hidden among the trees. These sounds made the little girl's heart pound. Toto walked close to her side and did not even bark in return.

Suddenly, there came a terrible roar, and a great Lion bounded into the road. With one blow of his paw, he sent the Scarecrow and the Tin Woodman spinning.

Toto, now that he had an enemy to face, ran barking toward the

Lion, and the great beast had opened his mouth to bite the dog, when Dorothy, fearing Toto would be killed, and heedless of danger, rushed forward and slapped the Lion on his nose as hard as she could, crying, "Don't you dare bite Toto! You ought to be ashamed of yourself, a big beast like you, to bite a poor little dog!"

"I didn't bite him," said the Lion, rubbing his nose.

"You tried to," she retorted. "You're a big coward!"

"I know it," said the Lion, wiping a tear from his eye with the tip of his tail. "It is my great sorrow. Danger makes my heart pound. Perhaps if I had no heart, I should not be such a coward."

"Have you brains?" asked the Scarecrow.

"I suppose so. I've never looked to see," replied the Lion.

"I'm going to the Great Oz to ask him to give me some," said the Scarecrow, "for my head is stuffed with straw."

"And I'm going to ask him for a heart," said the Woodman.

"And I'm going to ask him to send Toto and me back to Kansas," added Dorothy.

"Do you think Oz could give me courage?" asked the Lion.

"Just as easily as he could give me brains," said the Scarecrow.

"Or give me a heart," said the Tin Woodman.

"Or send me back to Kansas," said Dorothy.

"Then, if you don't mind, I'll join you," said the Cowardly Lion.

"You'll be very welcome," answered Dorothy. So they set off.

Soon they saw a great ditch dividing the road. They crept up to the edge to look over. It was very deep, with many big, jagged rocks at the bottom, and both sides were too steep to climb down.

"What shall we do?" asked Dorothy.

"I think I could jump over it," said the Lion.

"Good," said the Scarecrow, "you can carry us over on your back, one at a time."

The Scarecrow went first. Dorothy went next; with Toto in her arms, she climbed on the Lion's back, holding tightly to his mane. The next moment, she felt as if she was flying through the air; and then, before she had time to think about it, she was safe on the far side. Then the Lion went back and got the Woodman.

They walked along in the sunshine amid great clusters of scarlet poppies, which soon covered the yellow brick road. Now, the odor of many poppies together is so powerful that any who breathe it fall asleep, and if not taken away from there, sleep on forever.

Soon Dorothy felt she must sit down to rest and to sleep. But they would not let her do this, and kept on going until Dorothy's eyes closed and she fell among the poppies, fast asleep, with Toto beside her. The Scarecrow and the Woodman, not being made of flesh, weren't troubled by the flowers' scent. The Scarecrow told the Lion, "Run fast, and get out of this deadly flowerbed quickly. We'll bring Dorothy with us, but if you should fall asleep, you are too big to be carried."

So the Lion bounded forward as fast as he could. The Scarecrow and the Woodman picked up Toto and Dorothy and carried them through the great carpet of deadly flowers. They came at last upon their friend the Lion, lying fast asleep among the poppies.

The flowers had been too strong for the huge beast and he had given up, at last, and fallen only a short distance from the end of the poppy bed, where the grass spread in green fields before them.

"We can do nothing for him," said the Woodman, sadly, "for he is much too heavy to lift. We must leave him here to sleep on forever, and perhaps he will dream that he has found courage at last."

"I'm sorry," said the Scarecrow, "the Lion was a good comrade for one so cowardly. But let's go on."

They carried the sleeping girl to a pretty spot beside the river, far enough from the poppy field to prevent her breathing any more of the poison of the flowers. Here they laid her gently on the soft grass and waited for the fresh breeze to waken her.

As they stood beside the girl, the Woodman heard a low growl, and saw a wildcat running after a little field mouse. The Woodman raised his axe and cut the cat's head off. The mouse stopped and squeaked. "Oh, thank you, thank you ever so much for saving my life! I am the Queen of all the field mice." And many field mice ran up, exclaiming that they were glad to find her alive and well, and bowed deeply.

"This funny tin man," she said, "saved my life. So hereafter you'll obey his every wish. Is there anything you'd like now?"

"Oh, yes!" said the Scarecrow. "Please save our friend, the Lion, who's asleep in the poppy bed."

"A Lion!" cried the little Queen. "Why he would eat us all up!"

"Oh, no, this Lion is a coward. He says so himself," answered the Scarecrow. "Please send for all your subjects to come at once, and let each one bring a piece of string."

Then the Scarecrow instructed the Woodman to chop up some trees to make a cart that would carry the Lion. The mice came from all directions, and Dorothy was greatly astonished to wake and find herself surrounded by thousands of little mice looking at her timidly. But the Scarecrow explained everything and, turning to the dignified little Mouse, he said, "Permit me to introduce you to her Majesty, the Queen."

Dorothy nodded gravely and the Queen made a curtsey, after which she became quite friendly with the little girl.

Then the Scarecrow and the Woodman harnessed the mice to the cart using the strings they'd brought. When all the mice had been harnessed, they were able to pull it quite easily to the place where the Lion lay asleep.

After much hard work, the two managed to get the Lion up on the cart. At first, the little field mice, many though they were, could hardly stir the heavily loaded cart; but with the Woodman and the Scarecrow pushing and the mice pulling, soon they rolled the Lion out of the poppies to a place where he could breathe fresh air again.

The Queen Mouse said, "If ever you need us again, call out to us in the field and we shall hear you and come to your aid. Goodbye!"

"Thank you so much, and goodbye!" the friends answered, and away the Queen ran, while Dorothy held Toto tightly lest he should run after her and frighten her. Then they sat down beside the Cowardly Lion until he should awaken.

It was some time before the Cowardly Lion awakened, but when he did, he was very glad to find himself alive.

"Now we must journey on to the Emerald City," said Dorothy.

The country was beautiful, and now, green fences lined the road.

"Surely we are getting near the Emerald City," said Dorothy.

"Yes," answered the Scarecrow, "everything is green here, while in the country of the Munchkins, blue was the favorite color."

They spent that night with a farm family. The next morning they started out early and soon saw a beautiful green glow in the sky ahead. Yet it was afternoon before they came to the great green wall that surrounded the City. Before them, and at the end of the yellow brick road, was a big gate, studded with emeralds that glittered so in the sun that even the painted eyes of the Scarecrow were dazzled by their brilliance.

There was a bell beside the gate, and Dorothy pushed the button. The big gate swung slowly open, and they found themselves in a high arched room, the walls of which glistened with countless emeralds.

Before them stood a little man about the same size as the Munchkins. He was all in green from his head to his feet, and even his skin was of a greenish tint. At his side was a large green box. When he saw Dorothy and her companions, the man asked, "What do you wish in the Emerald City?"

"We came here to see the Great Oz," said Dorothy.

The man was so surprised at this answer that he sat down to think it over. Then he said, "I am the Guardian of the Gates, and since you demand to see the Great Oz, I must warn you: Oz is great and terrible. If you come on an idle or foolish errand, he might be angry and destroy you instantly. Now, you must put on the spectacles, because if you didn't wear them, the brightness and glory of the Emerald City would blind you. They're locked on, for Oz has so ordered it. I have the only key that will unlock them."

He opened the big box, which was filled with spectacles of every size and shape. All of them had green glass in them. The Guardian found a pair that would just fit Dorothy and put them over her eyes. Two golden bands fastened them around the back of her head, where they were locked on with a little key that was at the end of a chain the Guardian wore around his neck. Then he fitted spectacles on the others, and even on little Toto; all were locked with the key. The Guardian put on his own glasses, took a big golden key from a peg on the wall, and opened the gate to the Emerald City.

Dorothy and her friends were dazzled by the brilliance of the wonderful City: the houses and streets were all green marble, studded with emeralds. Even the rays of the sun had a green tint.

The Guardian of the Gates led them through the streets until they came to the Palace of Oz, the Great Wizard. A soldier stood at the door, dressed in a green uniform and wearing a long green beard.

"Here are strangers," said the Guardian of the Gates to the soldier. "They wish to see the Great Oz." The soldier bade them enter the hall and went to deliver their message to the Great Wizard.

When the soldier returned, Dorothy asked, "Have you seen Oz?"

"Oh, no," he replied, "I have never seen him. But I told him of your silver shoes and the mark upon your forehead, and he decided

to grant you an audience. Now I will have you shown to rooms where you may rest in comfort after your journey." He blew upon a green whistle, and at once a young girl, dressed in green with green hair and eyes, entered the room, and led them all to pretty green rooms. The next morning, the green maiden dressed Dorothy in a pretty gown made of green silk, then Dorothy added a green silk apron and tied a green ribbon around Toto's neck. Next, the green girl led them to the throne room of the Great Oz. They came to a great hall, and were shown into a big, round room with a high dome roof; every surface was covered with large emeralds. What interested them most was the big throne of green marble: in the center of the seat was an enormous Head.

As Dorothy gazed upon this, the eyes looked at her; and the mouth said, "I am Oz, the Great and Terrible. Who are you, and why do you seek me?"

It was not such an awful voice as she had expected to come from the big Head; so she took courage and answered, "I am Dorothy, the Small and Meek. I have come to you for help."

"Where did you get the silver shoes and the mark upon your forehead?" the voice demanded.

"The Witch of the North gave me the shoes, and kissed me to protect me from harm when she sent me to you. My house fell on the Wicked Witch of the East and killed her, and—" she replied.

"What do you wish me to do?" the Voice demanded.

"I want to go back home to Kansas, and my friends here, the—"

"Why should I do this for you?" the voice of Oz interrupted. "You have no right to expect me to help you unless you do something for me in return. You must kill the Wicked Witch of the West!"

"But I cannot!" exclaimed Dorothy, greatly surprised.

"You killed the Witch of the East and you wear the silver shoes, which bear a powerful charm. There is now but one Wicked Witch left in all this land, and when you can tell me she is dead I will grant your requests—not before."

The four friends were stunned at this answer. They had no wish to kill anyone. As each stepped forward to make his plea—the Scarecrow to ask for brains, the Tin Woodman for a heart, and the Lion for courage, each got the same answer. To obtain their hearts' desires, they must kill the Wicked Witch. Outside the fearsome throne room, they sadly resolved to begin their quest the very next morning.

The soldier with the green beard led them through the streets of the Emerald City until they reached the outer Gates. The Guardian unlocked their spectacles and put them back in his box.

"Which road leads to the Wicked Witch of the West?" asked Dorothy.

"There is no road," answered the Guardian of the Gates. "No one ever wishes to go that way."

"How then are we to find her?" inquired the girl.

"That will be easy," replied the man, "for when she knows you are in the Country of the Winkies, she will find you and make you all her slaves."

"Perhaps not," said the Scarecrow, "for we mean to destroy her."

"Oh, that is different," said the Guardian. "No one has ever destroyed her before, so I naturally thought she would enslave you, as she has all the rest. Keep to the West, where the sun sets, and you cannot fail to find her."

They thanked him and bade him goodbye, and turned toward the West, walking over fields of soft grass. Dorothy still wore the pretty silk dress she had put on in the palace, but now, to her surprise, she found it was no longer green, but pure white. The ribbon around Toto's neck had also lost its green color and was as white as Dorothy's dress.

The Emerald City was soon left far behind. As they advanced, the ground became rougher and hillier, and the ground was untilled.

In the afternoon the sun shone hot in their faces, for there were no trees to offer them shade; so that before night, Dorothy and Toto and the Lion were tired, and lay down upon the grass and fell asleep, with the Woodman and the Scarecrow keeping watch.

Now the Wicked Witch of the West had but one eye, but that was as powerful as a telescope. So, as she looked out from her castle and saw the little company in her country, the Wicked Witch became very angry; and she blew upon a silver whistle.

At once there came to her a pack of great, fierce wolves, and a flock of wild crows, enough to darken the sky.

"Go to those people," said the Witch to the wolves and the crows. "Peck out their eyes and tear them to pieces."

The wolf pack dashed away, and the crows after them. Luckily, the Scarecrow and the Woodman heard them coming. The Woodman seized his axe and the Scarecrow stood with his arms outstretched to frighten the crows. As the wolves attacked, the Tin Woodman swung his axe until forty wolves lay dead in a heap. The Scarecrow caught the birds by the neck and twisted them until the forty crows lay dead in a heap.

The next morning, they started again upon their journey.

Now this same morning the Wicked Witch looked out with her one eye and saw all her wolves and crows lying dead, and this made her even angrier; she blew her silver whistle. Straightaway, a swarm of black bees came to her. She ordered them to sting the strangers to death; the bees flew right to our friends. The Scarecrow said, "Take out my straw and scatter it over the little girl and the dog and the Lion." The Tin Woodman did this, and as Dorothy lay close beside the Lion and held Toto in her arms, the straw covered them entirely. Soon the bees came and flew at the Tin Woodman, breaking their stingers against the tin, without hurting him at all; and as bees cannot live when their stingers are broken, that was the end of the black bees.

Dorothy and the Lion got up and helped the Tin Woodman put the straw back into the Scarecrow again.

The Wicked Witch was furious when she saw her bees in little heaps like fine coal. She couldn't understand how her plans to destroy these intruders had failed; so she made up her mind what to do. She had a charmed Golden Cap; whoever owned it could command the Winged Monkeys three times. The Wicked Witch had used two orders already—but she saw no other way to destroy Dorothy and her friends. So she took the Cap, and spoke the charm. The sky darkened and a low rumbling was heard. There was a rushing of many wings, a great chattering and laughing, and the Witch was surrounded by a crowd of

Winged Monkeys. The biggest one flew close to the Witch and warned her this was her last summons.

"What is your third and last command?"

"Go to the strangers and kill all but the Lion—he's fit to work."

They obeyed. The Monkeys flew the Woodman high in the air and dropped him on sharp rocks. Some unstuffed the Scarecrow and put his clothes in a high tree. The leader flew to Dorothy, but saw the kiss of the Good Witch and knew he dared not harm her. So the Monkeys carried the Lion, Dorothy and Toto to the castle of the Wicked Witch.

The leader of the Winged Monkeys explained to the Wicked Witch, "We dare not harm the child, nor her dog. Your power over our band is now ended."

Then the Winged Monkeys flew away. The Wicked Witch was worried about the mark on Dorothy's forehead, for she knew it protected her from evil; and when she looked down and saw the silver shoes, she trembled with fear. But she saw in Dorothy's eyes that the child didn't know of the power the silver shoes gave her, nor the protection of the good Witch's kiss. So the Wicked Witch said to Dorothy, harshly, "Come with me; and see that you mind everything I tell you, for if you don't, I'll make an end of you, as I did of the Tin Woodman and the Scarecrow."

Dorothy followed her through the castle to the kitchen, where the Witch bade her clean the kettles and sweep the floor and keep the fire fed with wood. Dorothy went to work meekly, and the Witch went into the courtyard and tried to harness the Cowardly Lion like a horse; but the Lion gave a loud roar and bounded at her fiercely. After that, she took no food to the imprisoned Lion; and every day she came to the yard at noon and asked if the Lion was ready to be harnessed like a horse. And the Lion would answer, "No."

The Lion didn't have to do as the Witch wished because every night Dorothy brought him food after the Witch went to sleep. Then, he and Dorothy tried to plan their escape, but they could find no way out of the castle.

Now, the Wicked Witch longed to steal the silver shoes Dorothy wore, for they were very powerful, but the child only took them off at night and when she took her bath. The Witch was too afraid of the dark to go into Dorothy's room at night and her dread of water was greater than her fear of the dark, so she never came near when Dorothy was bathing. Indeed, the old Witch never touched water. One day, the Witch played a trick on Dorothy. She placed an iron bar (which she made invisible by magic) in the middle of the kitchen floor.

Poor Dorothy stumbled over it and fell; one of the silver shoes came off, and the Witch snatched it and put it on her own skinny foot. The wicked woman was greatly pleased, for one of the shoes gave her half the power of their charm, and Dorothy could not use it against her, even had she known how to do so.

The little girl grew angry when she saw she had lost one of her pretty shoes, and said to the Witch, "Give me back my shoe!"

"I won't," retorted the Witch, laughing, "for it is now my shoe, not yours, and some day I shall get the other one from you, too."

This made Dorothy so very angry that she picked up a bucket of water and dashed it over the Witch, wetting her from head to foot.

The wicked creature shrieked; and then, she began to shrink.

"See what you've done!" she screamed. "I'm going to melt away."

"I'm very sorry, indeed," said Dorothy, who was truly frightened to see the Witch actually melting away before her very eyes.

"I never thought a little girl like you would ever be able to melt me and end my wicked deeds. Look out—here I go!" With these words the Witch fell down in a melted shapeless mass and began to spread over the kitchen floor. Seeing that she had really melted away to nothing, Dorothy drew another bucket of water and threw it over the mess. She picked out the silver shoe, then swept it all out the door, and ran to tell the Lion that the Wicked Witch of the West was dead!

The Cowardly Lion was much pleased to hear that the Wicked Witch had been melted by a bucket of water, and Dorothy unlocked the gate of his prison and set him free. Dorothy's first act was to call together all the Winkies, who had long been the Witch's slaves, and tell them they were free.

There was great rejoicing among the yellow Winkies, for they had been made to work hard during many years for the Wicked Witch, who had always treated them with great cruelty. They kept this day as a holiday, then and ever after, and spent the time in feasting and dancing.

"If our friends, the Scarecrow and the Tin Woodman, were only with us," said the Lion, "I should be quite happy."

"Do you suppose we could rescue them?" asked the girl.

"We can try," answered the Lion.

So they called the yellow Winkies and asked them if they would help, and the Winkies said that they would be delighted to do all in their power for Dorothy, who had set them free from bondage. So she chose a number of the Winkies and they all started away.

They traveled that day and part of the next, until they came to the rocky plain where the Tin Woodman lay, all battered and bent. His axe was rusted and the handle broken.

The Winkies lifted him tenderly in their arms, and carried him back to the castle, where Dorothy asked if any of the Winkies were tinsmiths.

"Oh, yes; some of us are very good tinsmiths," they told her.

"Then bring them to me," she said. And when the tinsmiths came, she asked, "Can you straighten out

the dents in the Tin Woodman, and solder him together where he is broken?"

The tinsmiths looked the Tin Woodman over carefully and replied that they could mend him so he would be as good as ever. They set to work in one of the big rooms of the castle and worked for three days and four nights, hammering and bending and soldering and polishing the Tin Woodman, until at last he was straightened out. To be sure, there were several patches on him, but the tinsmiths did a good job. Meanwhile, another of the Winkies had made an axe-handle of solid gold and fitted it to the Woodman's axe, instead of the old broken handle.

When at last the Tin Woodman walked into Dorothy's room and thanked her for rescuing him, he was so pleased that he wept tears of joy. Her own tears fell thick and fast at the joy of meeting her friend again. As for the Lion, he wiped his eyes so often with the tip of his tail that it became quite wet, and he was obliged to go out into the sun till it dried.

"If we only had the Scarecrow with us again," sighed the Tin Woodman after Dorothy had finished telling him all that had happened.

"We must try to find him," said the girl.

So she called the Winkies to help her, and they walked all that day and part of the next until they came to the tall tree in the branches of which the Winged Monkeys had tossed the Scarecrow's clothes. The Woodman set to chopping it down. In a short time, the tree fell over with a crash and the Scarecrow's clothes fell out of the

branches and onto the ground. The Winkies carried them back to the castle, where they were stuffed with nice clean straw; and behold! here was the Scarecrow, as good as ever, thanking them over and over again for saving him.

Now that they were reunited, Dorothy and her friends spent a few happy days at the castle. But one day, the girl said, "We must go back to Oz, and claim his promise."

"Yes," said the Woodman, "I'll get my heart."

"And I'll get my brains," added the Scarecrow.

"And I'll get my courage," said the Lion.

"And I'll get back to Kansas," cried Dorothy. "Oh, let us start for the Emerald City tomorrow!" The next day they bade the Winkies goodbye. The

Winkies were sorry to have them go, and they had grown so fond of the Tin Woodman that they begged him to stay and rule over them. But finding they were determined to go, the Winkies gave Toto and the Lion each a golden collar; and to Dorothy they gave a beautiful bracelet. And to the Scarecrow they gave a gold-headed walking stick, to keep him from stumbling; and to the Tin Woodman, they gave a silver oil-can, inlaid with gold and set with precious jewels.

Dorothy went to the Witch's cupboard to fill her basket with food for the journey, and there she saw the Golden Cap. She tried it on her own head and found it fitted her exactly. She knew nothing about the charm of the Golden Cap, but she saw that it was pretty, so she made up her mind to wear it and carry her sunbonnet.

Then they started for the Emerald City. The travelers knew they must go straight east, toward the rising sun. But at noon, when the sun was over their heads, they realized they were lost in the great, barren fields. One by one, they lost heart—even Dorothy. She sat down on the grass and looked at her companions, and they sat down and looked at her, and Toto panted and looked at Dorothy as if to ask what they should do next.

"Suppose we call the field mice," she suggested. "They'll tell us the way to Oz." So they called out and in a few minutes the Queen and her subjects came running. The Queen of the mice asked how she could help them.

"Can you tell us where the Emerald City is?" they asked.

"Certainly," answered
the Queen; "but it is a great
way off. Why don't you use the charm
of the Golden Cap you wear to call the Winged Monkeys to help
you? They will carry you there in no time."

"I didn't know there was a charm," answered Dorothy in surprise.

"It is written inside the Cap," replied the Queen. "Don't be afraid;
they must obey the wearer of the Cap. Goodbye!" And she scampered out of sight, with all the mice hurrying after her.

Dorothy looked inside the Golden Cap and read the charm. Then
she put the cap back on her head and followed the instructions to
summon the Winged Monkeys. They heard a great chattering and
flapping of wings as the band of Winged Monkeys flew up to them.
The King bowed low before Dorothy and asked for her command.

"We wish to go to the Emerald City," said the girl.

"We will carry you," replied the King. So two Monkeys caught
her in their arms and flew away with her. Others took the frightened Scarecrow and the Tin Woodman and the Lion, and one little
Monkey seized Toto and flew after them. In no time at all, the odd
creatures set the travelers down carefully before the gate of the
Emerald City; the King bowed to Dorothy and the band flew away.

The Guardian of the Gates led the travelers through the City,
telling all that they had melted the Wicked Witch of the West. The
soldier with the green whiskers carried the news to Oz; but Oz made

no reply for several days. At last the Wizard sent for them to come to him, but the throne was empty. They kept close to the door and one another. They heard a disembodied Voice say solemnly, "I am Oz, the Great and Terrible. Why do you seek me?"

"We have come to claim our promises," said Dorothy.

"Has the Wicked Witch been destroyed?" asked the Voice, and Dorothy thought it trembled slightly.

"Yes," she answered, "I melted her with water."

"Dear me," said the Voice; "how sudden! Well, come to me tomorrow: I must have time to think."

The Lion thought it might be as well to frighten the Wizard, so he gave a large, loud roar, which was so dreadful that Toto jumped away from him in alarm and tipped over the screen that stood in a corner. As it fell with a crash they looked that way, and they saw a little old man, with a bald head, who seemed to be as much surprised as they were.

The Tin Woodman, raising his axe, rushed toward the little man, and cried out, "Who are you?"

"I am Oz, the Great and Terrible," said the little man, in a trembling voice, "but don't strike me—please don't!"

The friends looked at him in surprise and dismay.

"We thought Oz was a great Head," said Dorothy.

"No, you are wrong," said the little man, meekly. "I have been making believe."

"Making believe!" cried Dorothy. "Are you not a great wizard?"

"Hush, my dear," he said. "Don't speak so loud, or you will be overheard—and I should be ruined. I'm supposed to be a Great Wizard."

"And aren't you?" she asked.

"Not a bit of it, my dear; I'm just a common man."

"You're more than that," said the Scarecrow, in a grieved tone; "you're a humbug."

"Exactly so!" declared the little man, rubbing his hands together as if it pleased him. "I am a humbug."

"But this is terrible," said the Tin Woodman. "How shall I ever get my heart?"

"Or I my courage?" asked the Lion.

"Or I my brains?" wailed the Scarecrow.

"My dear friends," said Oz, "I pray you, think of me, and the terrible trouble I'm in at being found out."

"Doesn't anyone else know you're a humbug?" asked Dorothy.

"No one knows it but you four—and myself," replied Oz. "It was a great mistake my ever letting you into the throne room. Usually I won't see my subjects, and so they believe I am something terrible."

"But I don't understand," said Dorothy in bewilderment. "How was it that you appeared to us as a great Head?"

"One of my tricks," answered Oz. "Step this way, please, and I will tell you all about it." He led them into a small chamber behind

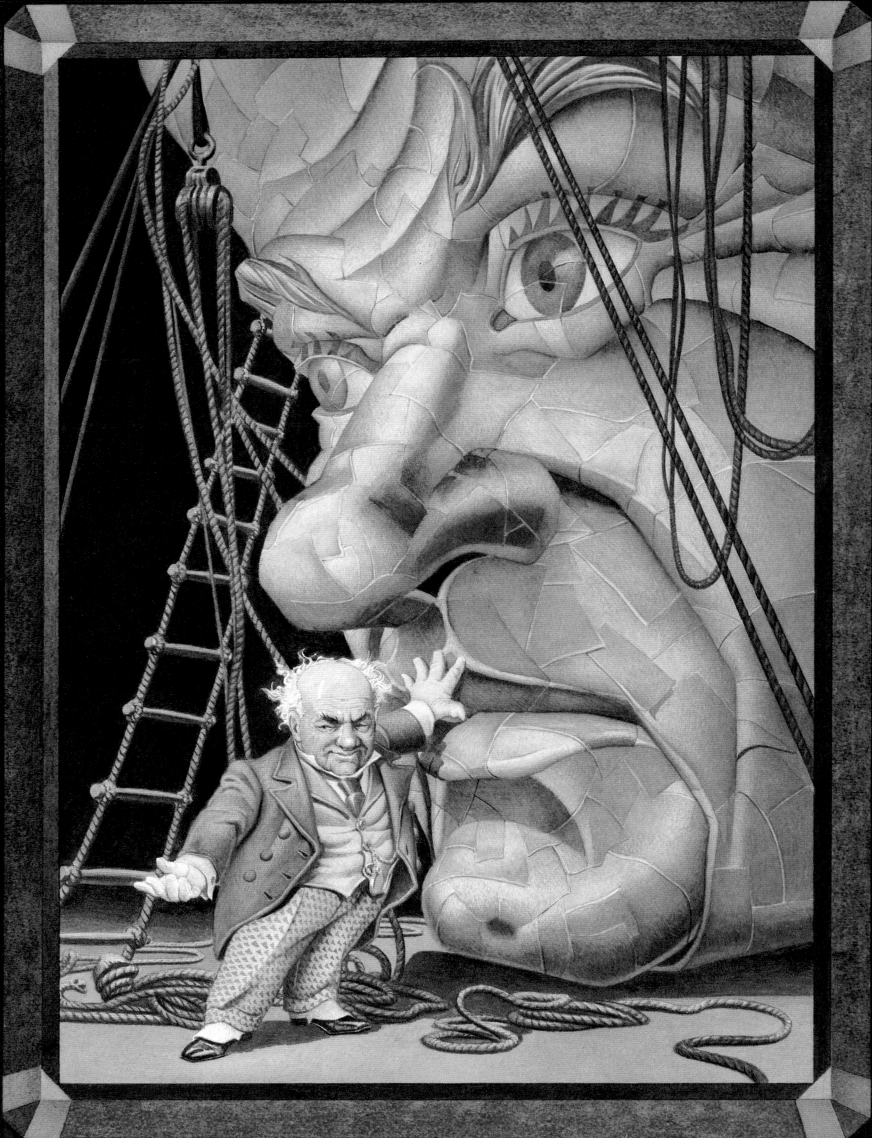

the throne room. In one corner lay the great Head, made out of many thicknesses of paper, and with a carefully painted face.

"This I hung from the ceiling by a wire," said Oz. "I stood behind the screen and pulled a thread, to make the eyes and mouth move."

"But how about the voice?" she enquired.

"Oh, I am a ventriloquist," said the little man, "and I can throw the sound of my voice wherever I wish."

"Really," said the Scarecrow, "you ought to be ashamed of yourself for being such a humbug."

"I am—I certainly am," answered the little man sorrowfully; "but it was the only thing I could do. Sit down, please, and I will tell you my story. I was born in Omaha—"

"Why, that isn't very far from Kansas!" cried Dorothy.

"No, but it's farther from here," he said sadly.

"When I grew up I became a ventriloquist, trained by a great master. After a time, I tired of that, and became a balloonist. I'd go up in a balloon on circus day, to draw a crowd of people. Well, one day I went up in a balloon and the ropes got twisted, so that I couldn't come down again. It went way up above the clouds. For a day and a night I traveled through the air, and on the morning of the second day I awoke and found the balloon floating over a strange and beautiful country. The balloon came down gradually; I found myself in the midst of a strange people who, seeing me come from the clouds, thought I was a great Wizard. Of course they were afraid of me, and promised to do anything I wished them to do.

"Just to amuse myself, and keep the good people busy, I ordered them to build this city, and my palace; and they did it all. Then I thought, as the country was so green and beautiful, I would call it the Emerald City, and I put green spectacles on all the people, so that everything they saw was green."

"But isn't everything here green?" asked Dorothy.

"No more than in any other city," replied Oz. "But when you wear green spectacles, of course everything you see looks green to you. My people have worn green glasses so long that most of them think it really is an Emerald City. I have been good to the people, and they like me; but ever since this palace was built, I have shut myself up and would not see any of them.

"While I had no magical powers at all, I soon found out that the Witches were really able to do wonderful things. The Witches of the East and West were terribly wicked, and had they not thought I was more powerful than they themselves, they would surely have destroyed me. So you can imagine how pleased I was when I heard your house had fallen on the Wicked Witch of the East. When you came to me I was willing to promise anything if you would only do away with the other Witch; but now that you have melted her, I am ashamed to say that I cannot keep my promises."

"I think you are a very bad man," said Dorothy.

"Oh, no, my dear, I'm really a very good man; but I'm a very bad Wizard, I must admit."

"Can you give me brains?" asked Scarecrow.

"You don't need them. You are learning something every day. A baby has brains, but it doesn't know much. Experience is the only thing that brings knowledge, and the longer you are on earth the more experience you are sure to get."

"That may all be true," said the Scarecrow, "but I shall be very unhappy unless you give me brains."

"Well," Oz said, with a sigh, "if you will come to me tomorrow morning, I will stuff your head with brains. I cannot tell you how to use them, however; you must find that out for yourself."

"Oh thank you—thank you!" cried the Scarecrow. "I'll find a way to use them, never fear!"

"But how about my courage?" asked the Lion anxiously.

"You have plenty of courage, I'm sure," answered Oz. "All you need is confidence in yourself. True courage is in facing danger when you are afraid, and that kind of courage you have in plenty."

"Perhaps, but I'm still scared," said the Lion. "I'll be very unhappy unless you give me courage that makes me forget I'm afraid."

"Very well; I'll give you that sort of courage tomorrow," said Oz.

"How about my heart?" asked the Tin Woodman.

"Why, as for that," answered Oz,

"I think a heart makes most people unhappy. You really are in luck not to have a heart."

"I will bear all the unhappiness without a murmur, if you will give me a heart," said the Tin Woodman.

"Very well," answered Oz meekly. "Come to me tomorrow and you shall have a heart."

"And now," said Dorothy, "how am I to get back to Kansas?"

"We shall have to think about that," replied the little man. "Give me a day or two to consider the matter and I'll try to find a way. There is only one thing I ask in return for my help—such as it is. You must keep my secret and tell no one I am a humbug."

They agreed, and went back to their rooms in high spirits. Even Dorothy had hope that Oz would find a way to send her home.

Next morning, the Scarecrow said to his friends, "I am going to Oz to get my brains at last. When I return, I shall be as other men are."

"I have always liked you as you were," said Dorothy simply.

He went to the throne room, where he rapped on the door.

"Come in," said Oz.

"I've come for my brains," said the Scarecrow, a little uneasily.

"Oh, yes; sit down," said Oz. "Please excuse me for removing your head, but I must put your brains in the proper place."

"That's all right," said the Scarecrow, "as long as it will be a better one when you put it on again."

So the Wizard unfastened his head. Then he took up some bran, mixed in many pins and needles, and filled the top of the Scarecrow's head with the mixture. He stuffed the rest of the space with straw. When he had fastened the Scarecrow's head on again, he said, "There now, I have given you a lot of bran-new brains."

The Scarecrow, both pleased and proud at the fulfillment of his greatest wish, thanked Oz warmly, and went back to his friends.

Dorothy looked at the Scarecrow curiously; his head was quite bulging out at the top with brains. She asked him how he felt.

"I feel wise indeed," he answered earnestly.

"Well I must go to Oz and get my heart," said the Woodman. So he walked to the throne room and knocked at the door.

"Come in," called Oz, and the Woodman entered and said, "I have come for my heart."

"Very well," said the little man, "but I shall have to cut a hole in your breast so I can put your heart in the right place." And Oz

brought a pair of tinner's shears and cut a small, square hole in the left side of the Tin Woodman's breast. Then, he showed the Woodman a pretty heart, made entirely of silk and stuffed with sawdust.

"Isn't it a beauty?" he asked.

"Oh, indeed!" replied the Tin Woodman. "But is it a kind heart?"

"Oh, very!" answered Oz. He put the heart in the Woodman's breast, and replaced the square of tin, soldering it neatly.

The Woodman exclaimed his gratitude and returned to his friends.

The Lion walked to the throne room and knocked at the door. "Come in," said Oz.

"I have come for my courage," answered the Lion as he entered.

"Very well," said the little man. He went to a cupboard and reached up to a high shelf, took down a square green bottle, and poured its contents into a green-gold dish. Placing this before the Cowardly Lion, the Wizard said, "Drink."

"What is it?" asked the Lion.

"Well," answered Oz, "if it were inside you, it would be courage. But courage is always inside one; so that this really cannot be called courage until you have swallowed it."

The Lion hesitated no longer, but drank till the dish was empty.

"How do you feel now?" asked Oz.

"Full of courage," replied the Lion, and went back to his friends.

Oz, left to himself, smiled to think of his success. "How can I help being a humbug?" he said. "They think I can do anything. But it will take more than imagination to get Dorothy back to Kansas."

For three sad days, Dorothy heard nothing from Oz, and she longed more than ever to get back to Kansas. Finally, Oz sent for her.

"Sit down, my dear; I think I have found the way to get you home. We each came to this country by air," said the Wizard; "I by balloon, you by cyclone. So I believe the best way to get across the desert will be through the air. I have plenty of silk in the palace to make a balloon, and we can fill it with hot air to make it float."

"We!" exclaimed the girl. "Are you going with me?"

"Yes," he answered. "Now, let's begin work on our balloon."

As fast as Oz cut the strips of silk into proper shape, Dorothy sewed them neatly together. First a strip of light green silk, then dark green, then emerald green. It took three days, but when it was finished, they had a big bag of green silk twenty feet long.

Then Oz painted it on the inside with a coat of thin glue, to make it airtight. He sent the soldier with the green whiskers for a big clothes basket, which he fastened with many ropes to the bottom of the balloon. When all was ready, Oz sent word to his people that he was going to make a visit to a great brother Wizard who lived in the clouds. The news spread rapidly and everyone came to see the wonderful sight. The Woodman chopped a big pile of wood and made a fire, and Oz held the bottom of the balloon over the fire so that the hot air would be caught in the silken bag. The balloon swelled out and rose into the air. Then Oz got into the basket and said: "I am now going away to make a visit. While I'm gone, the Scarecrow will rule over you. Obey him as you would me."

The balloon tugged at the ropes that held it to the ground, for the air within it was hot, making it so light in weight that it pulled hard to rise into the sky.

"Come, Dorothy!" cried the Wizard. "Hurry, or the balloon will fly away."

Toto had run after a kitten, but Dorothy found him and picked him up and ran toward the balloon. She was so close and Oz was holding out his hand to help her up when crack! went the ropes, and the balloon rose up in the air without the little girl.

"Come back!" she screamed from down below. "I want to go, too!"

"I can't come back, my dear." called Oz from the basket. "Goodbye!"

"Goodbye!" shouted everyone, and all eyes were turned upward to where the Wizard rode in the basket, rising farther and farther into the sky. And that was the last any of them ever saw of Oz, the wonderful Wizard, though the people remembered him lovingly, recalling that he'd built the beautiful Emerald City and left the wise Scarecrow to rule over them.

Dorothy wept bitterly at losing her chance to get home to Kansas again. The morning after the balloon went up with Oz, the four friends met in the throne room.

"If Dorothy would only be contented to live in the Emerald City," said the Scarecrow, "we might all be happy together."

But Dorothy, of course, wanted to go home to live with Aunt Em and Uncle Henry. The Scarecrow thought and thought and finally he said, "Why not call the Winged Monkeys, and ask them to carry you over the desert?"

"I never thought of that!" Dorothy put on the Golden Cap and spoke the charm to summon the band. Soon the Winged Monkeys flew in through an open window. The Monkey King bowed and said, "This is the second time you have called. What do you wish?"

"I want you to fly with me to Kansas," said Dorothy.

"We cannot," he said. "We belong to this country alone, and cannot leave it. We'll be glad to serve you, but we cannot cross the desert." He bowed to them, spread his wings and flew away.

Dorothy was ready to cry with disappointment. So the Scarecrow thought again, and finally he suggested they call in the soldier with the green whiskers. The soldier entered the throne room and they asked him how Dorothy might cross the desert. He suggested that perhaps Glinda, the good Witch of the South, might help.

"Glinda rules over the Quadlings," he explained. "The road to her castle goes straight south, but it is full of dangers to travelers. There are wild beasts in the woods, and a race of queer men who do not like strangers in their country."

When the soldier left, the Scarecrow said, "It seems, in spite of the dangers, that the best thing Dorothy can do is to ask Glinda to help her. If Dorothy stays here, she will never get back to Kansas."

"I shall go with Dorothy," declared the Lion, "for I

long for the woods and the country again. Besides, Dorothy will need me to protect her."

"That is true," agreed the Tin Woodman. "I, too, will go with her."

"When shall we start?" asked the Scarecrow.

"Are you going?" they asked in surprise.

"Certainly. If it was not for Dorothy, I should never have had brains. We'll go tomorrow morning," he said, "for it will be a long journey."

The next morning they all shook hands with the soldier with the green whiskers, who had walked with them as far as the gate. When the Guardian of the Gates saw them again he at once unlocked their spectacles, which he put back into the green box, and gave them many good wishes to carry with them.

"You are now our ruler," he said to the Scarecrow, "so you must come back to us as soon as possible."

"I certainly shall if I am able," the Scarecrow replied.

As Dorothy bade the good-natured Guardian farewell, she said, "I have been very kindly treated in your lovely city. I cannot tell you how grateful I am."

"Don't try, my dear," he answered. "We should like to keep you with us, but if it is your wish to return to Kansas, I hope you will find a way." He then opened the gate and they started upon their journey.

The sun shone brightly as our friends turned their faces toward the Land of the South. Dorothy was once more filled with the hope of getting home, and the Scarecrow and the Tin Woodman were glad to be of use to her. As for the Lion, he sniffed the fresh air with delight and pure joy at being in the country again, while Toto ran around them barking merrily all the time.

"City life does not agree with me at all," remarked the Lion, as they walked along at a brisk pace. "Now I am anxious for a chance to show the other beasts how courageous I have grown."

They turned and took a last look at the Emerald City. All they could see was a mass of towers and steeples behind the green walls, and above everything, the spires and dome of the Palace of Oz.

"Oz was not such a bad Wizard, after all," said the Tin Woodman, his heart rattling around in his breast.

"He knew how to give me very good brains," said the Scarecrow.

"If Oz had taken a dose of the same courage he gave me," added the Lion, "he would have been a brave man."

Dorothy said nothing. Oz had not kept his promise to her, but she forgave him. He was a good man, even if he was a bad Wizard.

The first day's journey was through the green fields and bright flowers. They slept that night on the grass, with nothing but the stars over them.

In the morning, they traveled on until they came to a thick wood. There was no way of going around it, for it seemed to extend to the right and left as far as they could see. So they looked for the place where it would be easiest to get into the forest.

The Scarecrow, who was in the lead, finally discovered a big tree with such wide spreading branches that there was room for the party to pass underneath. But just as he came under the first branches, they bent down and twined around him, and the next minute, he was raised from the ground and flung headlong among his fellow travelers.

This did not harm the Scarecrow, but he looked rather dizzy when Dorothy picked him up.

"Here is another space between the trees," called the Lion.

"Let me try it first," said the Scarecrow, "for it doesn't hurt me to get thrown about." He walked up to another tree, but its branches immediately seized him and tossed him back again.

"This is strange," exclaimed Dorothy.

"The trees seem to have made up their minds to stop our journey," remarked the Lion.

"I believe I will try it myself," said the Woodman, and, shouldering his axe, he marched up to the first tree that had handled the Scarecrow so roughly. When a big branch bent down to seize him, the Woodman chopped at it so fiercely that he cut it in two. At once the tree began shaking all its branches as if in pain, and the Tin Woodman passed safely under it.

"Come on!" he shouted to the others, "be quick!"

They all ran forward and passed under the tree without injury. The other trees of the forest did nothing to keep them back, so they decided that probably the first row of trees were the policemen of the forest, and were given this wonderful power in order to keep strangers out of it.

Later, in the forest, they came upon a gathering of animals, who appeared fierce but who were so impressed by the Lion's courage that they begged him to be their King. He promised to return once he saw Dorothy safely home.

The four travelers passed through the rest of the forest in safety; when they came out from its gloom, before them was a steep hill, covered with rocks. The Scarecrow led the way up the hill.

"Keep back!" A head showed itself over the rock and said, "This hill is ours. You may not cross it." From behind the rock stepped a short, stout man with a big head, flat at the top and supported by a thick, wrinkled neck. But he had no arms at all.

"I'm sorry not to do as you wish, but we must pass over the hill," the Scarecrow said, and he walked boldly forward.

As quick as lightning, the man's head shot forward and his neck stretched out until the top of the head struck the Scarecrow in the middle. He went tumbling down the hill. Then the head snapped back to the body. There was a chorus of boisterous laughter, and Dorothy saw hundreds of the armless Hammer-Heads upon the hillside.

The Lion gave a loud roar and dashed up the hill and again a head shot swiftly out, and the great Lion went rolling down the hill.

"Let's call the Winged Monkeys for help," suggested the Woodman.

Dorothy put on the Golden Cap and spoke the magic words. In an instant, the Monkey King stood before her and asked for her command.

"Carry us over the hill to the country of the Quadlings," answered

the girl. The Hammer-Heads yelled with vexation, and shot their heads high in the air; but they could not reach the Winged Monkeys, who caught the four travelers and Toto up in their arms and flew safely over the hill.

"This is the last time you can summon us," said the leader to Dorothy, "so goodbye, and good luck to you."

"Goodbye, and thank you very much," returned the girl.

They were now in the country of the Quadlings. The people were short, chubby, cheerful, and dressed all in red. The friends walked up to a beautiful castle. At the gates were three girls in red uniforms trimmed with gold braid; as they drew near, one girl asked why they had come to the South Country. "To see the Good Witch Glinda," Dorothy answered. The soldier girl took them to a room where they prepared themselves for their audience. When they were ready, they followed the soldier girl into a big room where the Witch Glinda sat on a throne of rubies. She was beautiful and young; her hair was a rich red and fell in flowing ringlets over her shoulders. Her dress was pure white, and her eyes were blue and kindly. "What can I do for you, my child?" she asked.

Dorothy told the Witch of the adventures they'd had. "My greatest wish now," she added, "is to go home, for Aunt Em must be worried." Glinda leaned forward, kissed the little girl, and told Dorothy she would send her home if Dorothy would give her the Golden Cap. Dorothy agreed and gave her the Cap. The Witch said to Dorothy's companions, "What will you do when Dorothy has left us?"

The Scarecrow planned to return to the Emerald City to rule over the people there; the Tin Woodman wanted to return to the land of the Winkies in the West, where he'd been asked to rule; and the Lion wished to return to the grand old forest where the animals had asked him to be their King. The Good Witch Glinda promised to use her three commands to the Winged Monkeys to get each to his separate destination. Then, having used up the powers of the Golden Cap, Glinda would give it to the King of the Monkeys, that they might be free evermore.

"But you have not yet told me how to get home," said Dorothy.

"Your silver shoes will carry you over the desert," replied Glinda. "If you had known their power, you could have gone back to your Aunt Em the very first day you came to this country."

"But then I shouldn't have had my brains!" cried the Scarecrow.

"And I shouldn't have had my lovely heart," said the Tin Woodman.

"And I should have lived a coward forever," declared the Lion.

"This is true," said Dorothy. "But now I want to go back home."

"The silver shoes," said the Good Witch, "have wonderful powers. They can carry you to any place in the world in three steps, and each step will be made in the wink of an eye. All you have to do is to knock the heels together three times and command the shoes to carry you wherever you wish to go."

Dorothy hugged and kissed her friends goodbye, and Glinda the Good stepped down from her ruby throne to give the little girl a goodbye kiss.

Dorothy thanked her for all the kindness she had shown to her friends and herself.

Dorothy now took Toto up solemnly in her arms, and having said one last goodbye, she clapped the heels of her silver shoes together three times.

"Take me home to Aunt Em!" she exclaimed.

Instantly she was whirling through the air, so swiftly that all she could see or feel was the wind whistling past her ears.

The silver shoes took but three steps, and then she stopped so suddenly that she rolled over on the grass several times before she knew where she was. At length, however, she sat up and looked about her. "Good gracious!" she cried.

For she was sitting on the broad Kansas prairie, and before her was the new farmhouse Uncle Henry built after the cyclone had carried away the old one. Uncle Henry was milking the cows, and

Toto jumped out of her arms and ran toward him, barking joyously.

Dorothy found she was in her stocking feet, for the silver shoes had fallen off in her flight and were lost forever in the desert.

Aunt Em had just come out of the house when she looked up and saw Dorothy running toward her.

"My darling child!" she cried, folding Dorothy in her arms and covering her face with kisses, "where on earth did you come from?"

"From the Land of Oz," said Dorothy gravely. "And here is Toto, too. And oh, Aunt Em! I'm so glad to be at home again!"